Knitting

Learn to Arm Knit Scarves & Blankets in Under 30 Minutes!

by Kitty Moore

Kitty Moore
ArtsCraftsAndMore.com

Table of Contents

Introduction

Ever tried to grip slippery knitting needles and then tried to manage the yarn while keeping a hold of the needles only to end up dropping the yarn or stabbing yourself with a needle? Knitting can be a challenge. And making it all work together to produce rows and rows of perfect stitches that will end up looking like a scarf or blanket can take a lot of time and patience.

Have you struggled with this traditional way of knitting and given up after finding yourself frustrated with ripping rows and rows of knitting as soon as you come across a mistake in your work?

If the answer to these questions is yes then this book is definitely for you. You will not need needles to create any of the projects in this book! You can make thick and cozy blankets, fun scarves, and even cozy carpets all with just some yarn and your arms. Arm knitting has become a very trendy hobby and you don't need any special skills or special equipment to learn it. You will be making fun items with your own two hands and your two arms.

This book will teach you how you can use nothing but your arms to make fantastic scarves and blankets in a fraction of the time that it takes you to knit the traditional way. Now now, wipe that look of disbelief off your face and pay careful attention to the following chapters. You will be given a window into a world that you probably never even knew existed.

In the time that it takes to watch your favorite show, you can start and complete your first scarf. Watching a movie you can create a fantastic blanket. This is a great way to add beautiful accessories to your winter wardrobe and to make beautiful handmade gifts for your friends and family that won't cost a fortune to make.

Let us get right to it then, and introduce you to the wonderful world of arm knitting!

Learn to Arm Knit Scarves

Scarves are essential for your winter wardrobe. Yes, they can be purchased relatively cheaply, but imagine the joy and satisfaction that you will get from making your own! You will be able to boast about making your own scarf with your own hands. And you will also have the freedom to create the scarf that you want in the colors and stitches that you want.

Before we get into the various stitches that you can use though and before you go absolutely crazy making arm knitted projects let's start with the basics. After all, the basics are the best foundation and once you have learned the basics you can start creating and designing all kinds of projects based on the stitches that you will learn.

The following tutorial will show you basic stitches and how to get started so that so you could have your first scarf finished in 30 minutes. Before you learn the basics however there are a few things that you should be aware of. The vocabulary of knitting is thankfully forgiving. It is not as in-depth as that associated with science or some other nasty crafts with buzzwords and lingo that are real tongue-twisters.

The following terms sum these up perfectly and getting your head and your tongue around them is really very simple.

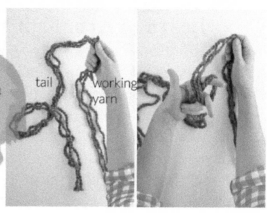

tail   working yarn

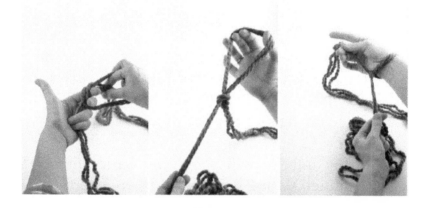

tail
working yarn

Terms You Need to Know

There are just four things in fact that you need to know when it comes to arm knitting, and these are the same for traditional knitting methods as well.

Cast On

Casting on is where you line up the stitches on your needle, or in this case your arm, in preparation for the actual knitting! Really, that's it! Seriously!

Rows

This is the development or progress of the actual knitting, each successive row that you knit, making the product longer! Again, that is it!

Cast Off

This is the final process when knitting, the part when you tie up the process by sealing your garment to avoid ripping and losing rows.

Skeins of Yarn

Skeins are balls of yarn. When you buy yarn in the store it comes already wound in skeins. But if you make your own yarn or buy from a fancy knitting shop the yarn might come loose and need to be wound into a skein. Most of the time the yarn you buy will already be in a skein though.

Materials

Yarn is the basic requirement. You will need two to three balls of yarn to begin with. There are different types of yarn available today, but for the purpose of this scarf, we recommend that you use the chunky variety! Actually, the bulkier or chunkier the yarn the better for the purpose of arm knitting!

You will also need a pair of scissors.

Of course, you will need your arms, but that goes without saying!

Directions

Before we get into the fun patterns that you can apply to your knitting, let us get a handle on the basics of arm knitting. Quickly, you will learn how to cast on, knit rows, and then cast off. What follows these directions is a window to a world of creativity that really is in your hands!

Casting on

1. Start by making a slip knot. Leave a 24-inch tail of the yarn, hanging from the end of the yarn that is not the ball!

2. Slightly tighten the slip knot over your right arm. This constitutes one stitch!

3. Grip the yarn using your left hand about 8 inches from the loop on your arm. Using your index finger and your thumb, separate the working yarn and the tail yarn by inserting these fingers into the yarn.

4. You then insert your right hand underneath the bottom strand of the yarn on your left thumb.

5. Using your right hand, grip the top strand of yarn over your index finger, pulling it through to create a loop!

6. Slide this loop over your right arm, tightening it slightly. You should now have two stitches on your arm. Repeat steps four to six until the required number of stitches is reached!

Knitting Your First Row

Once you have reached the requisite amount of stitches, you will have done your first row. Pull on this work gently, straightening it out!

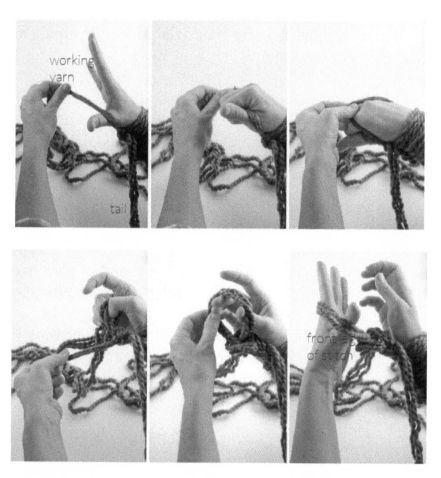

Twist loop 1/2 turn here to make the working yarn be the front leg of the stitch

See the front of stitch is the working yarn

tip:

To keep the fabric looking full, try to make the stitches as tight as you can while still being able to maneuver. Do this by grabbing the working yarn close to your left hand for the next stitch

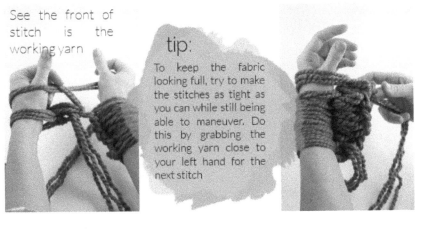

Knitting Your Second Row

1. Grasp the working yarn with the left hand and pull through the first loop on left arm, using your right hand to guide this loop off your arm.

2. Place the loop that you just created onto your right arm. This is one knit stitch made!

3. Repeat the first two steps until all the stitches have been worked and moved to the right arm.

4. Repeat the first and second row instructions until you reach the desired length!

Casting Off

Move all stiches to the right arm before you start to cast off. However, if you want to cast off from stitches on your left arm, simply reverse this process.

1. Knit first two stitches.

2. Pull the stitch that is closest to the elbow over the second stitch and guide this stitch off the left arm!

3. Knit one stitch-two stitches on the left arm. Repeat steps two and three until one stitch remains on the arm. Then you cut the working yarn, completely drawing it through the last stitch on your arm. Pull it tightly, and then secure!

tip:
cast off loosely
When binding off, keep the stitches loose enough to match the width of the stitches below. It's easy to make it too tight.

There you have it. Following these steps will produce your first scarf or at least a long piece of knitted work that you should be very proud of!

Let us now go through the quick guide for making a blanket with nothing but your arms and a few balls of yarn!

I have included a bonus just for you…

FOR A LIMITED TIME ONLY – Get my best-selling book "DIY Crafts: The 100 Most Popular Crafts & Projects That Make Your Life Easier" absolutely FREE!

Readers who have downloaded the bonus book as well have seen the greatest changes in their crafting abilities and have expanded their repertoire of crafts – so it is *highly recommended* to get this bonus book today!

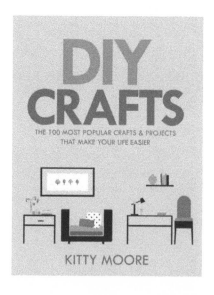

Get your free copy at:

ArtsCraftsAndMore.com/Bonus

Learn to Arm Knit Blankets

Blankets might seem like a daunting venture, especially if you are a novice knitter, but arm knitting a blanket is relatively simple, and quick.

Follow the instructions closely, and in under an hour, you will have a beautiful, chunky blanket!

Materials

- 3 skeins of bulky yarn

- Your arms

Choosing Yarn

When you are arm knitting you want to use the biggest and chunkiest yarns that you can find. Look for yarns that are tagged as being Bulky or Super bulky because they are the right size to create the projects that you want to make.

You might still want to combine several strands together to make a blanket or a rug even if you are using very thick yarn.

If you can't find the colors that you want in a Bulky or Super bulky weight you can combine strands of worsted weight yarn to make the yarn bulky enough to use in arm knitting projects.

Directions

You may not need to use all of the yarn unless you are making a really large blanket. The reason that you need 3 skeins is that the skeins will be combined to make a really thick blanket. You will use three strands as you go, as opposed to one or two. Note that you can create different looks by mixing things up with your yarn.

Arm knitting is easy once you get the hang of it. But you might have to practice for a few minutes until you get comfortable with this style of weaving. Because it is a chunky style it goes rather quickly. So if you are looking for instant gratification follow these instructions to create a beautifully knitted blanket in under an hour!

1. **To create your first row of stitches**

   Measure off some yarn to start with. Stretch out about 12-feet of extra yarn. Make a slip knot at this point. This knot needs to be large enough to fit your forearm just below the elbow. Slide this slip knot into your arm. Two strands of yarn will now be in front of you, your tail yarn and the working yarn, which comes off the ball directly. This 12-foot tail is what you will use to cast on your first row!

2. **Cast about 25 stitches**

   Although you can do more stitches if you want to make a larger blanket. This will give you a nice-sized lap throw, and depending on the size of your arms, or how much you stretch it, the blanket could be bigger or smaller. So, how do you cast on these stitches?

3. Use your arm and the slip knot

Take your finger and go under the yarn on your thumb. Stretch that yarn upwards, and loop it over the yarn on your finger. Then pull the yarn on your finger upward. This creates a stitch. Feed your hand through this loop, essentially casting the stitch onto your arm. Once you get it onto your arm, you tighten both strands of yarn. The stitches should be loose enough to move up your arm. Repeat this 25 times, but by all means, feel free to do more!

4. You are now ready to start adding rows

Push your excess tail yarn off to the side. You might not have much tail left, and you can always add it to your blanket later, at the end. Using the arm that has the stitches, grab the working yarn with your hand. Pull one stitch off your arm, and then pull the working yarn through this stitch. Put your opposite arm through this loop that you have just created. This is the first stitch of your new row!

5. Repeat this arm knitting

Until you reach the desired length. Use your lap as a guide. You should do at least 30 rows. It is now time to bind the blanket, and effectively wrap things up!

6. Your final row is started

As you did all the others once you have two stitches left take the stitch that is furthest from your hand, pass it over the other one and then right over your hand. Knit one more stitch onto your arm repeating the process. After you reach the end, cut the yarn and tie it in a secure knot!

You have just completed a blanket using nothing but your arms and you should be very proud of yourself!

Let us now talk you through a couple of creative stitches that you can learn once you are comfortable with this weaving technique.

Learn New Stitches

Different stitches make the scarf or blanket have a different appearance. Think of these stitches as the way in which your color your item, and you can color it with various stitches in various combinations. The most popular stitch is the purl stitch, and it is discussed briefly below!

Purl Stitch

The purl stitch is a common stitch, and chances are, if you have seen someone knitting before, they have been using a combination of plain stitching and purl. You do not need any special equipment to perform this!

Materials

- Super bulky yarn

- Your arms

Directions

1. Grab the working yarn with your right hand.

2. Bring the working yarn through the stitch in your right arm, while you keep the working end of the loop towards the front of your hand. Slip the stitch off the right arm.

3. Keep the working end of the loop to the front of your hand, and don't twist it, simply slipping the newly formed loop to the left arm.

You purl from the left arm by doing the following:

1. You have the working yarn in front of the work, inserting the right hand through the forward loop of the stitch on your left arm.

2. Grip the working yarn in your right hand, bringing it through the stitch on your left wrist, allowing the stitch on your left wrist to fall off!

3. Bring the stitch over the right wrist, while you keep the working end of the yarn to the back of the wrist!

Seed Stitch

This is a very rich and textured stitch. This stitch adds a lot of volume and texture to a project and the multiple colors make the stitch really stand out. This is great for scarves and items that you are going to wear.

Materials

- Several strands of yarn in different colors

- Your arms

Directions

1. It is created by alternating knits and purls, and purls and knits for every other row. It gives you a very rich, almost seed like look. Using as many strands of yarn as possible is best whenever you use these textured stitches, because with smaller holes, you can really take advantage of this richness.

I-Cord Stitch

In traditional knitting, this is used to make those decorative chords for wrapping presents or creating bows for dresses. Or it can have practical applications, for example, drawstrings on waist bands. In arm knitting, it creates a rope effect, for accessories like scarves.

Materials

- Yarn of your choice

- Your arms

Directions

1. Firstly, you cast on the amount of stitches that the pattern calls for. You then knit the first row as you would if you were traditionally arm knitting. Now, if you were knitting traditionally, you would just knit the stitches over to you other hand. With I-chord though, you need to bunch the fabric so that it forms a tube.

2. You do this by taking all the stiches from your one hand, and moving them over to your other hand, with the working yarn close to your elbow. Then you bring the yarn back over your stitches, and you knit the stitches as you would if nothing was different, and if nothing had changed. You would

knit them back over to your other hand as though you were knitting traditionally.

3. Give it a tug, and you will notice that you now have a tube-like fabric, because the stitches have basically fallen into each other. That is really it. You just continue to transfer the stitches over to the other hand, and repeat the process.

Cable Stitch

This is a very pretty stitch, and you can see that it is defined by cable-like patterns in your work, whether you are making a scarf, a pillowcase or a cowl!

Materials

- Thick yarn

- Your arms

Directions

1. Cast on your first row, as discussed in the first chapter on learning to arm knit scarves. Use the butterfly cast on method. Pass all the loops to your other arm. Hold on to your working yarn with the hand that has all the stiches on it now. Pass the yarn over this hand, with the working yarn still held firmly in your hand, and then move the stitches over your hand that has the stitches again, right over to the other hand that has no stitches on it now.

2. Repeat this process by passing the yarn, and therefore the stitches to the other hand. Then you bind off once you reach the desired length, and there you have it, a perfectly cable-stitched piece of work.

Garter Stitch

The garter stitch is also known as the knotted stitch. Unlike the plain and twisted stitches, which are knotted on just one side, the garter stitch is knotted on both sides.

This is a very cool stitch to use when you are creating fabrics that are reversible, because they will show knots on both sides. It is great for scarves and shawls, where people see both sides of the fabric that you are wearing. This is because these knots should look the same, depending on your level of skill!

Materials

- Yarn of your choice

- Your arms

Directions

1. You start by casting on, as you always do. This is the one step that remains consistent, no matter what stitch you plan to use subsequently. As said, casting on is discussed in the first chapter, where you can go and see how to do this. Chances are though, that by now, you have pretty much mastered the casting on process!

2. The yarn then goes from front to back, over your thumb, and you twist the stitch as you move it from

the right hand to the left hand. If you need a reminder on this, check the first chapter of this book. Note too that once you get the hang of this process, you might not even need to keep the yarn over your thumb for every single stitch. This is just a way to keep you oriented in the beginning.

3. Once you complete this first row of plain stitch, you will note that the knot is away from your body. For the next row, you bring the yarn back to front over the thumb, moving the stitch across from the left to the right without twisting it this time, and there you have it. When you are working from your right hand onto your left, you are just doing plain stitch, and when you work in the opposite direction, from left to right, you are going to do what is essentially a twisted stitch.

    Note: The twisted stitch is really the same as the plain stitch, without the twist. Note too that the working yarn is always towards you. You will soon fall into a rhythm with how you need to do it, doing this technique in a way that feels comfortable to you. You just continue this technique until your fabric reaches the desired length.

4. When you put the fabric down, you should have knots on the one side of your fabric. When you flip the fabric over, low and behold, you have the same knots on the opposite side as well. You have just created a completely reversible piece of fabric, one that you can grow and grow until you have a scarf, a

shawl, or even a blanket, depending on how many stitches you cast on to start with!

5. All you do now is bind it, casting off and securing it with a knot, and then you can boast to all your friends about your newfound skill!

Tips for Arm Knitting

Arm knitting is really an interesting technique, and you can master it very quickly with a little practice. There are ways to make your arm knitting more enjoyable however, and that can result in interesting and unique creations.

The following are just a few tips that can add serious value to your experience:

1. The thickness of scarves can be manipulated by simple using more strands. Using more strands results in a thicker final product!

2. You can also fix mistakes, much the same as you would with traditional knitting. If you are not using all your threads while knitting, for example, you can actually un-knit the row that you are working on. All you have to do is relax, slide the old stitch back on your opposite arm, and gently pull out the stitch from the current row.

3. You can correct tension too, by straightening it out after every few rows, much the same like you would when you work I-cord! This is important, because the irregularities of arms make your stitches uneven and funny looking. Try also to place the stitches in the same position each time!

4. You can also stop mid-project, if the phone rings or you have to answer the door. This is usually not necessary though, because these projects can

be completed relatively quickly. But when you do, all you need to do is slide the stiches onto a broom stick or another large stick. When you are ready to resume your knitting, you simply slide the stitches back onto your arm.

5.   You can make large loops in your knitting too, or keep it tight and compact by simply loosening or tightening your stitches.

These are simple tips that you can add to your arsenal of arm knitting tools, and they can go some ways to make you a better arm knitter. There are many patterns too that you can use when arm knitting, and once you have your head around the basics, you can start to see how your hands work together to create some of the patterns in the following chapter!

1. 30 Minute Scarf

Materials

- Bulky yarn

- Scissors

- Tapestry needle

Directions

1. Cast on 10 stitches. Work one row of knit stitch. Count your stitches.

2. Keep working rows of knit stitch until your scarf is at least 52 inches long. Cast off.

3. Sew the ends of the scarf together with the tapestry needle to create an infinity scarf.

2. 30 Minute Throw Blanket

Materials

- 11 skeins of bulky or super bulky yarn

- Scissors

- Your arms

- Tapestry needle

Directions

1. Cast on 18 stitches.

2. Knit 32 rows or until the blanket is as big as you want.

3. Cast off. Weave in ends.

3. Cuff Bracelet

Materials

- Bulky weight yarn or several strands of worsted weight yarn worked together

- Arms

- Button

- Needle

- Thread

Directions

1. Cast on 4 stitches. Knit 6-10 rows in Seed stitch.

2. Cast off. Sew the button to one end of the cuff.

3. Fasten the bracelet around your wrist by inserting the button end of the cuff into one of the loose stitches on the other end.

4. One Skein Infinity Scarf

Materials

- 1 skein super bulky weight yarn

- Arms

- Tapestry needle

Directions

1. Cast on 5 stitches. Knit the first row in plain knit stitch. Knit the next row in Garter stitch.

2. Knit the next row in knit stitch. Keep going alternating stitches in each row until the scarf is as long as you want it.

3. Cast off. Sew the ends together and weave in the edges.

5. Cozy Winter Boot Cuffs

Materials

- Bulky weight yarn

- Arms

- A button

- Tapestry needle

- Sewing needle

- Thread

Directions

1. Cast on 4 stitches.

2. Knit a piece that is long enough to around your calf. Cast off.

3. Sew the button to one end of the cuff. When that is complete you should be able to button the cuff easily by slipping the button through one of the stitches at the other end of the work.

6. Striped Scarf

Materials

- 3 skeins of super bulky yarn in different colors

- Arms

Directions

1. Cast on 12 stitches. Knit 3 rows.

2. Change colors by cutting the yarn that you are using and joining it to another skein of yarn in a different color. To do that take a different color of yarn and knot it to the end of the first color tightly. Trim the ends and continue to knit.

3. Change colors every 3 rows. Knit the scarf until it's long enough to be doubled over your head. Cast off. Join the ends of the scarves by tying the tail from casting on to the tail from binding off.

7. Easy Knit Pillow

Materials

- 2 skeins super bulky yarn

- 1 16" square pillow form

- Tapestry needle

Directions

1. Cast on 16 stitches. Knit one row using Garter stitch or Cable stitch.

2. Keep knitting until the finished piece is 32" long. Cast off. Fold the piece in half.

3. Use the tapestry needle and the tail of the cast on row to sew the two short sides shut. Insert the pillow form. Sew the last side shut.

8. Big and Cozy Blanket

Materials

- 12 skeins of super bulky yarn

- Arms

Directions

1. Cast on as many stitches as you need to make the blanket the size you want it to be. To make a 50" wide blanket you will need about 70 stitches.

2. Knit the blanket in garter stitch. Keep going until it's about 60" long.

3. Cast off. Weave in the edges or trim them.

9. Easy Shawl

Materials

- 5 skeins of worsted weight or bulky weight yarn

- Arms

- Scissors

Directions

1. Use all 5 strands of yarn together to knit the entire shawl. Always make sure you have all 5 strands on your arms while you are knitting. Cast on 28 stitches. Knit one row.

2. Knit the first 2 stitches together, then knit one stitch in each stitch until you get to the last 2 stitches in the row. Knit those 2 stitches together. Repeat for 11 rows.

3. Knit 2 stitches together then the next 2 stitches together for one row. Cast off.

10. Knit Necklace

Materials

- 4 different colors of bulky weight yarn

- 2 large beads

- Tapestry needle

- 2 O rings

- Necklace clasp

- Jewelry Wire

- Jewelry Pliers

Directions

1. Hold all 4 strands of yarn together. Cast on 2 stitches. Use the I-Cord stitch to knit the necklace as long as you want it to be. Cast off.

2. Use the needle to thread the tail yarn through the beads. Put one bead on each side of the necklace.

3. Braid the tails. Attach an O ring to the braid, one on each side. Use the jewelry wire and pliers to attach the clasp to the necklace. Wear the necklace.

Check out Kitty's books at:

ArtsCraftsAndMore.com/go/books

11. Color Block Blanket

Materials

- 6 skeins of super bulky weight yarn in different colors

- Arms

- Scissors

Directions

1. Cast on 18-20 stitches or however many you need to make the blanket the size you want. Knit 10-20 rows in one color.

2. Switch colors by cutting off the working yarn stand about 6 inches away from the end of the last stitch. Tie a new color to the end of the working yarn tightly. Keep knitting.

3. Knit another 10-20 rows in the second color. Switch colors back to the original color or use a 3rd color. Keep knitting and switching colors until the blanket is the right size. Cast off.

12. Fringed Evening Wrap

Materials

- 4 -6 skeins of bulky weight yarn

- Arms

- Scissors

Directions

1. Cast on 10 stitches.

2. Knit 10-20 rows to make the shawl the length that you want.

3. Cast off.

To Make Fringe:

Cut 3 pieces of yarn that are about 16 inches long. Thread all three pieces together through one stitch at the end of the scarf. Double them and tie them in a large knot. Repeat that process in each stitch.

13. Bathing Suit Cover Up

Materials

- 4-6 skeins of bulky weight yarn

- Arms

Directions

1. Hold all the strands of yarn together and use them as if they were one strand. Cast on 30 stitches or however many you need to make it long enough to go around your hips. Knit a row with a loose knit stitch.

2. Knit another row with a loose knit stitch. Knit the first two stitches together and continue knitting down the row until you get to the end. Knit the last two stitches together. Repeat for the next 10-12 rows or however long you need to make the piece so that it reaches your ankles from your waist.

3. When it's long enough knit the first two stitches of the next row together. Then knit the next two stitches together. And the next two. Until the row is finished. Cast off.

14. Thin Statement Scarf

Materials

- 2 skeins bulky weight yarn or 4 skeins of worsted weight yarn worked together

- Arms

- Tapestry needle

Directions

1. Cast on 6 stitches.

2. Knit 10-20 rows until the scarf measures the size you want. Cast off.

3. Use the tapestry needle and the tails of the yarn to sew the ends of the scarf together to make an infinity scarf.

15. Super Chunky Cowl

Materials

- 4 skeins of super bulky yarn

- Arms

- Tapestry needle

Directions

1. Work with all 4 strands of the super bulky yarn together as one strand to make a massive chunky strand. Cast on 6 stitches.

2. Work 10-12 knit rows until the cowl fits you.

3. Cast off. Fold the knitted piece in half and sew the ends together to make a cowl.

16. Simple Accent Scarf

Materials

- 5-10 skeins of worsted weight yarn

- Arms

Directions

1. Cast on 10 stitches.

2. Use I-Cord stitch to knit as many rows as you need to make the scarf about 50" long.

3. Cast off. Add fringe if you want to make it a little more dramatic.

17. Throw Rug

Materials

- 12 skeins of super bulky yarn in any color combination you like

- Arms

- Large tapestry needle

Directions

1. This rug is made of several squares sewn together. To make the basic square cast on 12 stitches. Knit 12 rows.

2. Cast off. Repeat this process to make as many squares as you need in the colors that you want to use.

3. Sew the squares together in any pattern you like to make a complete rug.

18. Tee Shirt Infinity Scarf

Materials

- 6-10 old tee shirts, depending on size

- Scissors

- Arms

- Tapestry needle

Directions

1. Break down the tee shirts by cutting them into long strips that are about an inch wide. Tie the strips together to make a thick yarn.

2. Cast on 10 stitches. Use I-Cord stitch to knit 10-20 rows until the scarf is as long as you want it.

3. Cast off. Sew the ends of the scarf together.

19. Thick Cozy Vest

Materials

- 6-8 skeins of super bulky yarn

- Arms

- Large tapestry needle

Directions

Front of Vest: (make two)

1. Cast on 6 stitches.

2. Knit 8 rows or the amount needed to make it fit.

3. Cast off.

Back of vest:

1. Cast on 12 stitches.

2. Knit until the back is the right length.

3. Cast off. Sew the two front pieces to the back, leaving openings for your arms.

20. Market Bag

Materials

- 2 skeins super bulky yarn

- Arms

Directions

1. Cast on 8 stitches.

2. Knit loose rows until the piece measures about 25".

3. Cast off leaving extra-long tails. Braid the tails to make the handles for the bag.

Note: If you don't have enough tail left to braid to make the handle you can cut long pieces of yarn, braid them, then sew them to the bag to make the handles.

Conclusion

Arm knitting is quick, both to learn and to perform. You will get hours of pleasure from creating these radical patterns that offer you a mostly doable alternative to the traditional needles and yarn type weaving. You will enjoy this experience, and as you get more and more comfortable with this technique, you will find your creativity growing as well.

Invest the time necessary to learn how to arm knit, and you can then set about adding spice and variety to your wardrobe. You can even make your own gifts for friends and loved ones, or maybe, just maybe, you can turn this into a business.

Whatever your reasons for taking on arm knitting, the rewards of this new skill are many. Yes, there is a quick turnaround time for arm knitting projects, but you will get hours and hours of satisfaction from really putting your hands into it!

Happy Arm Knitting…

Last Chance to Get YOUR Bonus!

FOR A LIMITED TIME ONLY – Get my best-selling book "DIY Crafts: The 100 Most Popular Crafts & Projects That Make Your Life Easier" absolutely FREE!

Readers who have downloaded the bonus book as well have seen the greatest changes in their crafting abilities and have expanded their repertoire of crafts – so it is *highly recommended* to get this bonus book today!

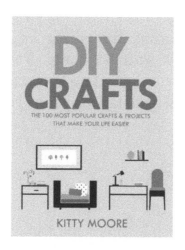

Get your free copy at:

ArtsCraftsAndMore.com/Bonus

Final Words

Thank you for downloading this book!

I really hope that you have been inspired to create your own projects and that you will have a lot of fun crafting.

I do hope that you and your family have found lots of ways to fill lazy afternoons or rainy days in a more fun way.

If you have enjoyed this book and would like to share your positive thoughts, could you please take 30 seconds of your time to go back and give me a review on my Amazon book page!

I really appreciate these reviews because I like to know what people have thought about the book.

Again, thank you and have fun crafting!

Disclaimer

No Warranties: The authors and publishers don't guarantee or warrant the quality, accuracy, completeness, timeliness, appropriateness or suitability of the information in this book, or of any product or services referenced by this site.

The information in this site is provided on an "as is" basis and the authors and publishers make no representations or warranties of any kind with respect to this information. This site may contain inaccuracies, typographical errors, or other errors.

Liability Disclaimer: The publishers, authors, and other parties involved in the creation, production, provision of information, or delivery of this site specifically disclaim any responsibility, and shall not be held liable for any damages, claims, injuries, losses, liabilities, costs, or obligations including any direct, indirect, special, incidental, or consequences damages (collectively known as "Damages") whatsoever and howsoever caused, arising out of, or in connection with the use or misuse of the site and the information contained within it, whether such Damages arise in contract, tort, negligence, equity, statute law, or by way of other legal theory.

Lightning Source UK Ltd.
Milton Keynes UK
UKHW011156131220
374972UK00002B/242